A NOTE TO PARENTS ABOUT BEING BULLIED

Almost every adult's collection of childhood memories includes situations in which he or she encountered a bully. Needless to say, these memories are seldom fond ones. Indeed, many adults consider their encounters with bullies to be some of their most traumatic childhood experiences.

The purpose of this book is to explain why people become bullies so that potential victims will not personalize the bully's misbehavior. In addition, the book teaches children how to deal with bullies.

Most of the time it is a good idea for children to confront their fears. This is not always the case with bullies. Many times it is smarter to walk away from a bully or to avoid him or her altogether.

If your child is in a situation in which he or she can not avoid or escape a bully, you need to intervene. Your child's maturation process does not require getting beaten up by a bully. Neither does it require standing up to one. The main goal is to get through childhood without becoming a bully's victim. There are a variety of ways to accomplish this goal. The best solutions are the ones that your child and you formulate together.

This book belongs to:

DMC RI#1

Published by Scholastic Inc.
90 Old Sherman Turnpike, Danbury, CT 06816.

SCHOLASTIC and associated logos are trademarks and/or
registered trademarks of Scholastic Inc.

ISBN 0-7172-8578-2

First Scholastic Printing, October 2005

A Book About
Being Bullied

by **Joy Berry**

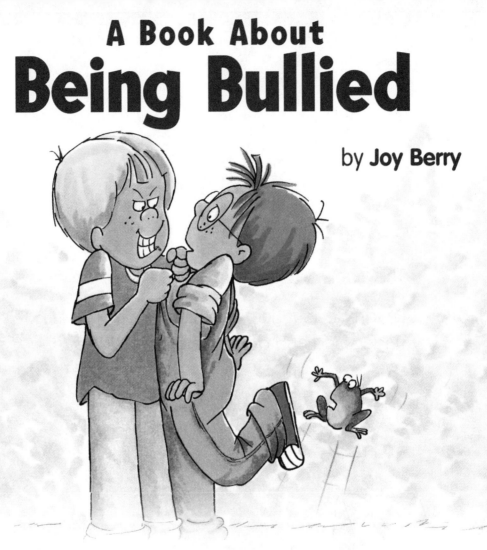

SCHOLASTIC INC.

New York Toronto London Auckland Sydney
Mexico City New Delhi Hong Kong Buenos Aires

This book is about Sam and Brad.

Reading about Sam and Brad can help you understand and deal with **being bullied.**

Bullies are people who act tough and like to fight.

Bullies like to frighten or hurt people who are smaller or weaker than they are.

Some people become bullies because *they feel inferior.* They feel that they are not as good as other people.

Bullies act tough and fight so they can feel that they are as good as or better than other people.

Some people become bullies because *they need attention.* They want people to notice them.

Bullies act tough and fight so people will notice them.

Some people become bullies because *they are frightened.* They are afraid other people might hurt them.

Bullies act tough so people will fear them and not bother them.

THESE KIDS ARE BIGGER THAN I THOUGHT THEY WERE. I'D BETTER ACT TOUGH SO THEY WON'T BOTHER ME!
HUMPH!

Some people become bullies because *they are angry.* They want to show their anger when something upsets them.

Bullies express anger by being mean and fighting with other people.

You are being bullied when someone:
- tries to control you or
- tries to frighten you into doing something.

I'VE DECIDED TO PLAY WITH YOU GUYS... ONLY WE'RE GOING TO PLAY WHAT I WANT!
UH... G-G-GREAT!
THIS KID IS AS FRIENDLY AS A RATTLESNAKE.

Being bullied can upset you. It can make you angry.

There are things you can do to avoid being bullied.

Treat bullies the same way you treat other people. *Be kind to them.*

Even bullies find it hard to be mean to a kind person.

Sometimes kindness does not stop bullies.

Stay away from bullies if being kind to them does not help.

Bullies cannot bother you if you are not around them.

Ignore bullies if you have to be around them.
- Do not look at them.
- Do not listen to them.
- Do not respond to them.

Bullies are less likely to bother you if you do not pay attention to them.

Confront bullies if it is impossible to ignore them.

- Face them. Look into their eyes.
- Tell them you do not want to be bullied.
- Tell them to leave you alone.

Walk or run away from bullies if they insist on fighting.

Bullies cannot fight with you if you are not around.

Get help if bullies keep bothering you.

Talk to your parents, teacher, or baby-sitter. Ask for help in handling bullies who are bothering you.

No one likes to be bullied. You can avoid being bullied by handling bullies the right way. It is up to you.